All the Wealth And Splendor

D.E. Ritterbusch

ISBN: 978-93-6354-973-9

First Edition: 2025
Rs. 200/-

Cyberwit.net
HIG 45 Kaushambi Kunj, Kalindipuram
Allahabad - 211011 (U.P.) India
http://www.cyberwit.net
Tel: +(91) 9415091004
E-mail: info@cyberwit.net

Printed at Repro India Limited.

ACKNOWLEDGMENTS

Grateful acknowledgment is made to the following publications in which these poems originally appeared and to the editors who subsequently reprinted these poems in their journals or anthologies.

BORDER CROSSING: *Homily; F=MA*

CANDLELIGHT POETRY JOURNAL: *Pansophy*

CAPE ROCK: *A Cold Nip*

DEADLY WRITER'S PATROL: *Warrior's Lament*

EDIFY FICTION: *One Helluva Life*

FLAR (Fredericksburg Literary & Art Review): *Millinery; The Carpenter's Lament*

FREE VERSE: *Winter in Brussels*

LAKE SUPERIOR STATE UNIVERSITY BLURB: *Heaven and Earth Conjoined*

MAGAZINE.SCINTILLAPRESS.COM: *Human Terrain*

NEW VERSE NEWS: *The Slight Difference of Things*

SCAPEGOAT REVIEW: *Doing a Binky*

SCHUYLKILL VALLEY JOURNAL: *Still Life: Lamentations of the Nude*

SOUTH BOSTON LITERAY GAZETTE: *Repairman Lamentations*

SQUALORLY.COM/POETRY: *Lamentations of the Body*

VERSE WISCONSIN: *An Economy of Characters*

WEST TEXAS LITERARY REVIEW: *The Natural World*

WFOP POETS' CALENDAR: *All the Wealth and Splendor; New Recipe; The Blouse; What It's Like*

WINGLESS DREAMER: *Wife in Winter*

WLA, wlajournal.com: *After a Reading of War Poems, the Signing of Books; Human Terrain*

CONTENTS

13 WAYS OF LOOKING AT SCHRÖDINGER'S CAT

I The cat is dead.

II The cat is alive.

III The cat is alive and dead at the same time.

IV Your wife will want to shake the box to discern the state of the cat. Tell her she cannot do this. Touching the box is not allowed. Rules are rules, and the rules of this thought experiment are fixed.

V The cat, according to the Many Worlds Theory, is alive in a vast number of worlds climbing an elaborate array of cat trees that almost mimic, in their configuration, a Feynmann diagram.

VI In Many Worlds the cat is as dead as any cat can be and has been buried in an infinite number of pet cemeteries almost always without a cosmologist to read the last rites.

VII The cat is beloved of the Creator and sits upon his lap purring loudly as the multiverse decoheres. The Creator denies being responsible for the creation of uranium, its properties of decay.

VIII If the dead cat and the live cat have wave functions that are interfered with, and it would not take much to do so, say a drop of cream falls from a container sneaked close to the box by a well-meaning cat lover, and that drop of cream still has an atom of strontium 90 left over from all those atomic tests in the desert, then perhaps, possibly, despite all the belief strictures on predestination, not even the most omniscient of gods will know what will happen inside the box.

IX The box is locked, cannot be opened—ever. The pin code containing an almost infinite number of digits has been misplaced. You may guess as you wish. Whatever.

X The box is no longer a toy for the cat to play in, and the cat has grown to dislike human beings intensely. It finds all their speculations as absurd as the nine lives nonsense that plagues the real world of cats.

XI Eminent physicists have refused to place a black cat in the box. Figure that one out.

XII Your wife will say the cat does not deserve someone such as you.

XIII

VINTAGE

Browsing a vintage bookstore,
stacks musty as old books are,
I found an antique collection of poems,
an early edition, 1891,
Palgrave's Golden Treasury.

Pressed between its pages,
between one lyric and another,
a flower, a pale daffodil
from another age

I imagine almost no one
presses a small flower
or four-leaf clover
between the pages of anything
any longer

My mother, in pages of
Emily Brontë's novel,
the edition read in her youth,
must have placed
a small, delicate plume
of blue larkspur
between the pages
in remembrance of some
wondrous moment

When I went through her books,
the blue plume fell into my lap

Remembrance, the flowered fragrance
of crystal perfume bottles
on her makeup table,
the scent still lingers
as does the scent of that pressed blossom

What lies between the words, the story,
and what story lived,
presses always against the heart

TESTAMENT

If I grow to be as deaf as the moon,
I wish my memory filled with *Turandot*,
the aria *Nessun Dorma*,
and with the sounds of poets reading
not to an audience, but to themselves.

If I am going to leave— so many
things undone— I want that drawer
of keys, many from cars owned
years and years ago, keys to doorways
unopened in decades, a skeleton key to the attic,
to a garage door always hard to open or close,
emptied. Melt them down
to make one key
opening to what you love the most.

If there is anything after,
I trust it needs some restoration or repair;
I've resurrected vintage cars, old houses,
art deco appliances that were designed to last a lifetime,
a pleasurable aesthetic that still draws the eye.
I will need something to make useful and lovely again.

For those I should have loved better,
know that love is still there,
now in greater abundance than then,
and any regret was a fault

of circumstance and the wicked dance
of time. I've been blessed
with fortune and grace
as munificent as rain.

THE SLIGHT DIFFERENCE OF THINGS

Cloudy and a few drops of rain—
not unusual for November
in Philadelphia; sometimes
the row houses go on forever
in that hazy, particulate light, and no one
walking pays much attention, eyes focused
on the patterning ground. So when
a young woman stops a couple
on the street and asks, *Where's the veterans'*
hospital? The man replies, *Over there,*
three blocks, turn right, the clinic
is right there, can't miss it; you can
take your pet there any time
during the day or make an appointment.
The woman turns away, says thanks,
a look in her eyes of misunderstanding,
misdirection, maybe traffic noise,
street music, inattention carried
in the air like ash or smoke,
or maybe veterinary hospital
and veterans' hospital sound so much alike
in the spin of the moment, the way
we want to hear, thinking the decent
thing about everyone, goodness
flowing like a rainbow of oil
in the rainy streets: just so

careless distractions order the day
as everyone walks apart, rain
chilling even the best intentions,
collars turned-up, shoulders hunched
with casual, unconsidered, indifference.

DOING A BINKY

On a very warm evening in summer
one of the rabbits in my backyard
turns over on its back, legs spread open
luxuriating in the cool, un-mowed grass.
My ex-wife, friend of my current wife,
has come to visit. We sit on the back porch,
a glass of wine in hand. She says, "This *is*
delightful, the rabbit so expressly happy."
I want to say, "If you had done that
level of luxuriating we'd probably still
be married," but the wisdom that comes
with marriage prevents any acerbic observation
to be anything other than suppressed.

Next night, several rabbits are out
biting heads off some of the perennials.
Their brilliant colors overload the landscape:
scabiosa, prunella, dianthus, although we know them
as blue note, summer daze, and neon star.

My wife joins me on the back porch,
chemo drugs coursing throughout
her body, a colorful babushka, like a field
of flowers, covers her bald head.
We watch a young rabbit race around
the yard. It does a binky and then another.
A sibling catches the spirit, races
to the fence line, one binky after another,
the leaping twist for joy repeated

as the most fashionable dance turn.
Another joins in and there are three rabbits
doing binkies, never a thought of farmer McGregor
or the mangy coyote that enjoys city life.
I put an arm around my wife's waist
as we stand watching their joy: "We'll be doing
binkies in no time," I say, "One binky after another.
All our days filled with binkies."

THERE IS NO TITLE FOR THIS

What happened
is still happening

Who you were
is still there
beyond the fence line

Living again,
under the night sky,
the winter moon
on pale snow

The quiet visits you again:
It is the same restful quiet
that brought you here

The place you started from,
the place you will end things
the place forward and back
that opens, closes, opens, closes

THE WARM SCENT OF VIET NAM

Along the Southern shore
racks of drying fish
send the perfume of nuoc mam
into lungs almost breathless in the heat,
and that carafe of water—
a few jasmine blossoms floating,
filling the room where winning
and losing at love lingers:
the smell of rice cooking,
oil heated in the alleys,
incense in the temples,
spirals burning overhead—
a curl of fragrant ash
falls with the delicacy
of a lotus blossom
to the floor below.

We're told memory and scent
are intertwined like lovers—
the strongest connection, a reification
of experience and yet,
and yet there is that loss,
the unifying code that defines us:
sweat on her shoulders,
the love in her eyes all lost
in the clarity, the disparity, of that scent,
memory a pale flower, a stick
of incense burning down the dark.

THE THRILL

I loved the thrill of the strike,
rod twisting in my hand,
line ripping out of the reel, drag
set for a long fight. My heart leaped
at the wild mystery of that fish,
rod bent almost to breaking.
That grand mystery,
what lay below the iron-dark water.

I don't relish it now, even though
long ago I changed and fished barbless.
Still, I want nothing from the depths,
the mystery shall remain so.

My canoe on still water
welcomes the morning calm,
sunlight above the tree line:
I wish only to be warmed,
my vest soaking up the sun.

A loon calls from across the lake.
A moose and her calf come down
to the water. I would look up
at the eagle soaring above
if only the sun were not shining so bright.

THE STORY OF ART

Everybody makes crap paintings—at some point.
—Damien Hirst

At the Barnes, Renoir room after room,
endless soft nudes, then oddly a nostalgic cottage
in the woods, *Environs de Briey,*
a small canvas that jars sensibility
like Soutine's painting of a flayed
rabbit. *It's like a Kincaid cottage*
without the lights on, I say to Irish,
and she replies, laconically, *Artists don't always*
have a great day. We've all had days
like Renoir's, a definitive mediocrity
swelling the hours.

Personally, I haven't had a great day
in a very long time: reams of wasted paper, wasted words,
litter bedroom and office, fill box after cardboard box.
I think of the bulbous-gray mass of organs
I stumbled over this morning as I stepped
off the porch, last night's hunt by the cats,
half-eaten rabbits, mice, and voles.
Could be worse, I say mumbling, fumbling wasps
and flies away from the remains—
art, soft nudes, rabbit guts, an enviable
still life: any more and I'd be sorely ashamed.

—for Jane Irish

THEATRES OF WAR

It is like an Ibsen play,
the fourth wall removed,
modern theatre although
there is so much silence, surprisingly,
no one speaking, almost no one
alive to speak, just sounds: irritable,
scrunching sounds of probing, poking,
digging through rubble and ruin,
through piles of household debris.

A disquieting familiarity
moves through the streets
like soldiers mopping up.

It seems we've moved across our stage,
the latest theatre of our absurd;
a mangy dog, gaunt, hungry, pitiable,
sniffs through, and you wish him luck,
though not so much
that he might find some sustenance
half-roasted, carved, or charred.

Après Les Théâtres du Grand-Guignol
the clever stage a nihilistic fit
while all the rest are witness to this shit.
    Though some, their faces turned away,
    may faint or vomit at this play,
    others quite more deeply love
    this high-tech decadent display.

So, there is a virtuous beauty in destruction.
Our history is of building temples on ruins.
Good comes of evil; wickedness begets
chaste energy—proportionately. Think of all that
scrabbling over loose precipitate.

But getting back to Ibsen
in our moralistic play:
front walls all gone, blown out
from every house along this street,
edifices standing on three legs,
a doll's house where the furniture
tells the story, the lives of those who lived
there: a wooden table in the kitchen—
one may surmise lively conversations
over dinner; the nursery visited
by parents looking down into a crib,
the crib nestled against a back wall; their
backs are turned to the audience in this play
in strident violation of dramatic rules.

But *all this* is violation, plumbing leaking
into the flat below, ruptured
pipes, strands of wire hanging,
shorting in the breeze, ash wafting
into lungs of those searching, looting,
a smell of burn, char fallen to the street,
crunching with plaster fallen. It is good
theatre in a Nietzschean way, though perhaps
that is in error; surely there are philosophers
since who know better. Adorno? Russell?
Heisenberg? Family pictures still hang
on the walls still standing.

The families themselves are nowhere
to be found, as if the actors have left
our stage, the drama, this last act, over and done.
No one comes out to take a bow;
the dog, unconcerned with our attention,
lopes to exit, stage left.

STOCHASTIC OOZE

(Barrier Tunneling)

It is explained
that possibility
within the realm of particle physics
allows for the passage
of one's automobile
from inside the garage
to outside, passing through
the walls as if they are not
even there, offering not the slightest
diffidence or impediment.

Such is the nature of the universe—
a divine conceit, a cosmology of jokes,
from the master trickster:
octopi have detachable penises
that search for pleasure on their own,
and bumble bees explode
on orgasm as if sitting on a live grenade,
remains splattered across
the windshield of the world.

Sometimes, when I can't find my car,
at the ballpark or in the parking lot
at the County Fair, I believe it moved,
transitioned from one state of matter to another,
and if God can do that
then why not transform my Ford wagon

into a Lamborghini Diablo?:
so, there I am, wandering from
aisle to aisle, looking not for my Taurus
but a flaming red throaty Diablo
proving the error of everyday logic
though such error may yield revelation,
a celebration of wishful nonsense;
still, I submit, even the imagination has limits.

However, let's suggest another possibility:
that you and I, love, pass through one morning
upon waking, finding ourselves lost
in the pleasurable physics of our transformation,
shapeshifting after all these years,
now on the other side of that impenetrable wall
leaving behind everything we've been used to—
the way we are to each other, worn out
like an old coat, threadbare, buttons
missing, yet we dare not throw it away
as we should have so many seasons ago.
And there we are, all pleasure regained,
your smile at my touch, my kiss,
because anything is possible, again.

NARRATOLOGY

Where's the story here? the editor asks
somewhat caustically, conditioned
to push the reject button
with every submission, every conversation
supporting one work or another.
Where's the story? **The story,** as if narrative
were everything—and yes often it is,
the story enough to carry it through,
but a moment's instance, some flash
of understanding, a satori touch,
and there we are. Maybe not
wisdom for the ages, but

one sharp, explosive glimpse, as when one sees
a dimension in string theory never
envisioned before: there, gone in an instant,
an afterimage dissipating in the fading
afterglow. **The story**, one might suggest,
lies in a string of such perceptions,
little drama, few characters, and the setting
just one outlying synapse sparking
very like some solitary neutrino
passing through a heavy water bath
almost impossible to detect.

ONE HELLUVA LIFE

Each morning, for half a century or more,
my grandfather walked downstairs
to coffee and eggs, the daily paper,
but on this one morning, a morning
like any other, he fell, tumbled down
to the landing below and broke his hip.
After surgery, a long hospital stay,
weeks of physical therapy that made but
little progress on recovery, he was placed
in a nursing home, a small room overlooking
a parking lot. Months later he would say,
standing at the window, staring out,
looking at the barren landscape below,
"This is a helluva life."

Often, I would take my grandmother to visit him.
She would stand by his bed and
banter with him the way she had
for sixty years: when you've been together
that long you can weather just about
anything, or can you? Perhaps such
anguished loss is worse than losing a child
or a favorite granddaughter who takes her own life
for no reason anyone can think of,
and the minister's words— *Everything*
happens for a reason known only
to God— fall flat as a cherished
flower bed after a storm of summer hail,
stems broken, petals beaten and scattered

across the lawn. She had taught me to hold
a snapdragon, to open its mouth
showing the perfect joinery
of a word and its experience.

On that first drive back to her home
leaving her husband to nurses
and caregivers other than herself,
she reflects over a lifetime,
saying, "There's so little time,
cuddle as much as you can,"
her language quaint as a doily.
I wonder if ever in her life
she used the phrase *having sex* or even
making love, but I knew she and grandfather
had a long life of cuddling;
you could feel the love between them
as they danced into their eighties.
As a sign of this love, they slipped cards
to each other to strengthen their hands
as if to say *We've been dealt a good life,*
but I'll make yours even better.

I drop her off, collect the mail,
go inside to make sure
she'll be ok. We talk to fill the empty space,
the time; we reassure each other, embracing
the lie he'll come home soon. When I leave,
she says, "Remember what I told you;
cuddle with Patricia, there's so little time."

I get into my car, sit there a minute, start

the engine and slowly back out of the drive.
I doubt we'd ever talked about sex but once,
when I was young, dating a girl my grandmother
disapproved of— *You be careful,* she said,
That girl will get you in trouble. Some girls
trick you into marrying them if you don't
watch out, the only cautionary tale
she'd ever ventured, letting me make
all the mistakes I could without reproof.

That night I searched Patricia's eyes
for the grandmother she'd become,
her crow's feet had deepened, her eyes
still a violet blue. We lay together,
my arm around her waist, cuddling all night long
as dragons roared, and lightning struck fire,
our garden drenched, and the antirrhinum
opened their mouths to the rain.

PSALM

When I search for you
in a crowd of shoppers,
I see a woman who looked like you
years ago, all that youthful grace
walking from aisle to aisle
in the supermarket.

But then I notice your coat;
you are looking at an array
of vegetables, the colors vibrant
and strong. Somehow my mind lurches
and spins from decade to decade
and I see you as you were, as you are,
years worn perfect as they pass.

PANSOPHY

When I was youthfully ignorant
of elemental properties and laws,
I took an iron rod and held it
in a fire; when the minutes passed,
and the rod didn't glow, I believed it cold
and grasped the end covered with ashes
in my hand, leaving a long white mark
across my palm, along the length of my thumb.
No homespun remedies, neither butter nor ice,
could cure that thought betrayed.

The lesson never changed,
so I've learned what not to touch
what not to observe, as the things that never glow
burn hottest, and any life thrown in
could sizzle and steam a large lake dry.

PALIMPSEST

I argue
and erase the argument

Yesterday is unforgiven
in its loss, retiring to a null set

Today will not join hands
with any construct not of its own choosing

An image bears fruit,
fades in sunlight like a prayer rug

All these signs and symbols
and the memory of masks

Surely it is time,
time bending to will

And curving as if to a singularity,
all love converging to a still point

A morning's feathers beneath an oak
betoken a desperate flight

I trace a feather across my hand,
feel its breath asking remembrance

In reverent silence a morning-glory opens—
Its color lasts the day

MY DAUGHTER READING LATE

Secretly, silently, her hand traces the page
as she lies in bed, one lamp lit
shadowing her face. Rock stars
postered on her bedroom walls,
a doll dressed in Victorian ribbon,
(skirt billowed wide as the shelf she sits on),
a menagerie of soft-furred friends,
all look on, vigilant, protective, as if ready
for any intrusion. Her world swallows time,
so much to be learned in a single day.
She memorizes theorems, axioms, postulates
until a bark-brown moth flies to the lamp.
She drops the page, remembers that tiny bat
caught in her room a few years before, windows
open, screen askew on a warm summer night.
The bat flew wildly around the ceiling's
circumference frightened by her father's predation.
Heart beating hard from my pursuit,
the untamed terror rested on her bedroom wall.
We closed the prison of a large, glass jar
over the quivering felt of its wings,
wing bones like tiny fingers, its nose
a licorice black. She held its sure release,
carried it carefully out back to a yard
brimming with insect sounds, a few fireflies
lighting the lawn. Quickly it was lost
in the web of branch overarching the house.
Now, sometimes, she watches bats circle
the night sky, wing to insect, vectors

sharp as figures on a page of geometry
problems, lines and angles scripted
on the Prussian blue, but tonight
her reading stops: a bat clings
to the window screen beside her.
She welcomes it like a cherished friend
who stops by simply to see if things
are going well, to see if everything's all right.

NOTEBOOK

Supposedly
        supposedly
language changes
        over time into another
not just clichés pronunciations
        extended meanings
all denotations become
        connotative
as the many worlds shift
        and morph
now a good friend
        next the enemy
of one’s existence
        distance is everything
meaning illusory
        if a proton were slightly
heavier it would decay into a neutron
        making life impossible
and one more syllable
        spoken one more letter
added one more word
        given to the lexicon
draws all our days together
        pulls all our days apart

RESTORATION WILDLIFE

Old houses locked up, boarded up,
abandoned for a long time,
have hundreds of flies
at their windows, denying light
in the attic, crunching underfoot
in an upstairs bath; its window
overlooks an overgrown backyard.
So many flies cling in their death
to the glass, the entire pane
lies covered with fly cack.
Spiders long dead have left webs
filled with their prey; a slight wind
through the sash and uneaten flies
move in their web as if alive.

Sweeping their carcasses up,
insect dust filters past my mask,
settles in my lungs, and it is a long
and ugly job to vacuum the remains;
their brittle wings break,
lift above the floor, and escape
into every crevice, every
inaccessible place.

I find a mummified squirrel
between joists, feathers for someone's bed,
and the skeletal remains of mice;
a few purloined trinkets rest
among the brittle bones.

There is mold on the attic rafters,
mildew on the basement walls,
a leak unchecked. Millipedes
stage a convention. I use so much bleach
the basement smells like a swimming pool.

Somehow, in a day or two,
the flies are back, returning to their cemetery
the way infirm elephants (knowing they are at the ends
of their lives) trek to their sacred, ancestral graveyards
to lie down and die.

Long ago it was thought
flies rose spontaneously
from rotten meat under glass—
biopoiesis a likely explanation
since they seem to erupt from nothing
in this fecund and perilous place:
mourning dove droppings drip from the transom,
something races past the corner of my eye
along a baseboard in the parlor.

If there were a belfry there would be bats.
No belfry but the bats come anyway;
they fly in at night, cling to the walls,
circle the ceiling and deposit guano on the floor.
I nail temporary plywood sheathing
over the broken window panes.
The house in *Psycho* looks more livable.

There is dog piss smelling up a closet,
cat urine saturates carpet in the living room;
after the carpet's removed the urine

is found to have saturated the hard maple floor.
I use a biological decontaminant to eat up
the urine, adding even more critters to the mix.

When I cut into woodwork saturated with cat piss
the stench makes me gag; I expect maggots
to disgorge from my throat.

Something has been living in the duct work,
its remains undecipherable.

Books and magazines left behind
are filled with silverfish
swimming through the pages;
they scatter when I thumb through
this unwanted lore, and they are there
in old copies of *Playboy* hidden
by teenagers, along with a weed pipe
above the rafters: they crawl lovingly
over the breasts of the centerfold.

The basement door is so gouged up
either a large dog or small child
has been imprisoned there
clawing to get out.

Plaster dust chokes the musty air,
lath springs back with a vengeance,
and, as the days warm, the odor
of death fills the house.
Under the front porch, the corpse
of a raccoon sheltered for winter
decays and putrefies the air.

I pull it out with a rake, double
bag it for the trash. I sense vultures
impatiently circling overhead
awaiting a free lunch.

Family members come by
to check the progress, seldom stop
to lend a helping hand. They walk
from room to room, gush that it will be
beautiful, the architecture stunning,
but they joke this job will kill me,
and more than likely I will not be here
to see it when it's done, such enjoyment
left to future generations, my corpse
just one more addition to the tally.

A wasp's nest has been abandoned,
a new residence located in the soffits.

I am a generous man, a live and let live
philosophy. I avoid them and expect the same,
but they do not reciprocate this kindness
and when I am stung, my Jainist beliefs
are tossed, and I wage chemical warfare
to their almost complete annihilation.

Nests of carpenter ants threatening to pull
the house down meet a similar fate.

A sun-warmed window
in the kitchen, the dirty window
above the sink, dead mice underneath,
has hundreds of flies clinging,

hundreds to be flushed to the city sewer.

I watch a funnel of iridescence
swirl down the drain, pray
for a long, cold winter,
thick ice sheeting the glass.

MYTHOS

Among many, there is the myth
of progress

Things get better over time,
the lives, the circumstances

But the marvel is that
change is not progress
yet perceived as such
a comfort for us all

Progress: a simple-minded jester,
and the jokes

humorless

Or, to find humor,
demonize it

Either way, anthropomorphize this conceit
for no good reason or any reason at all—

I mention this because I believed

I mention this because, looking back,
I wanted more

Perhaps, that is the way it should be

Everything left pretty much as it was

undying grace, undying remorse,
relentless the undying

NO ONE WOULD BELIEVE

No one would believe
who they were
once, so long ago;
who they were recedes
into an unremembered past
like a paper boat
floating down this narrow stream
swollen with late spring rain

I come here often,
watch leaves float and spin,
note small fish
lazily swirl their fins
to avoid the current's
insistent tug

I too have the feeling
of those small fish
under this carved out bank

Protection of sorts
but from what?
Nothing precarious awaits
beneath an overhanging branch

All is quiet: I fashion
a boat from a page torn
from a book I'd written,

a minor thought,
written as if it mattered

It sails down the cool, never-ending stream
that washes into something larger

Perhaps some gathered ancestors
may read what is found there
plucking the sodden boat from the water

Perhaps someone tired,
resting on the flowering bank
in need, sustenance withheld,
will take note of the missive
passing by and retrieve it,
and read it, a curiosity nourished,
or, more likely, as the current flows,
will knowingly let it pass.

NO EXPLANATION NECESSARY

Music in the morning—
Coltrane, the blues, Lady Day
and Lester Young, and then suddenly,
slowly, imperceptibly the rush is gone.
And she just stopped calling,
just like that, the music stopped
and her heartbeat wasn't there,
hand no longer tracing a syncopated
beat under her blouse
along the small of her back—gone
like a dove on the sill, looking in
puzzled by my stillness
looking out and suddenly, the eyes of
our time averted it is gone,
and today of all days a plastic bag
from the grocery store, hanging in
the tree outside this window for weeks,
filling with the winter wind like a kite,
and today with no wind it is gone
leaving the bare
branches to sort it out for themselves
and when I see her next, she says
I'm sorry, and *You must have taken it*
hard, and I say *You don't owe me*
any explanation as she walks away
and I think only of the morning
filled with jazz riffs, a blues song
you'd trade all your love for, all
the joy sucked out like the microtonal wind

and I know love is as blind as Blind Boy
Fuller and Blind Willie McTell and Blind
Lemon Jefferson, and still, I did not
see that coming.

HOMILY

In high school, an English teacher
who had little to say of any importance,
who bragged of reading every night
before bedtime, as if literature
were to be taken like a sleeping pill,
a woman who corrected grammar
with a dispassionate unconcern for any ideas
the student might dare to express,
who made an assembly line dullness
her way of life and resented our
blasphemous, exuberant youth
said something that stayed and stayed
from the moment she said it:
Ask your parents if they're doing
what they set out to do. So few
ever get a real chance.
Maybe she was expressing her own displeasure,
maybe she recognized her own limitations
as we all do when the time comes
for honest introspection.
Maybe she knew few were capable
of learning any lesson she taught,
perhaps only the years could do that.
I wonder sometimes at the rest of the class,
how many took her words to heart,
how many lie in bed at night,
their faces turned to the wall, a book
dropped from the hand, feeling
some loss of control, perhaps recalling

the classmate who skidded into a tree
leaving us all to reflect
on whatever went wrong.

HEAVEN AND EARTH CONJOINED

Viet Nam 2000

Only twenty minutes from the city
down a tributary of the Saigon River
sharp-winged birds dart and call,
evening's only break in the stillness—
reeds sway back and forth
as a bird alights; a golden carp
rises to the surface,
breaks the silent green
of the river.

In evening shadows, you move
as slender as the reeds, movement
of your arms as when the bird alights—
our embrace like that of the carp
breaking through the dark,
rising to the warm breath of heaven.

I AM LAZING AROUND A HOTEL POOL

I am lazing around a hotel pool,
the sun warm, the sky endless
and a young woman lies next to me,
me a middle-aged monster of a man
always raging at the current state of cosmic affairs
proving the inutility of reflection.
She lies at an acute angle, sunning
herself, enjoying her youthful beauty,
the sensuousness of life, beauty gushing
across the landscape. She adjusts
her bikini bottom, lifts the waistband,
and I see the beauty of her black curly hair,
bikini poised just briefly above that gentle mound
before her waistband snaps back,
but that glimpse lasts forever, a classical
painting hung on the wall of memory,
an aesthetic never to go extinct
no matter the passage from one
continuum to another. Marcel Duchamp
wanted paintings of *frequency*
while I find myself thoroughly
disgruntled at getting older, my acceptance
or avowal prescribing
recollection as my only salvation.

Once, a young woman showered after
we had made love, her period
soaking the bed sheets, and she bent over
to wash her sinewy legs and a gush

of blood flowed down those legs,
the water washing that crimson flow
to a bloody pink, and I loved her
for that moment, that moment
all I have left, a few random fluctuations,
lines of force transecting memory and desire.

What is there but an accumulation of images—
my role reduced, mere audience worthy
of little attention— that can take the place
of that sensuous, sun-filled ardor
and profound longing, that simple glimpse,
an eidetic image, and I, limited by
my imagination, can think of nothing,
nothing ever so sublime.

. . .

If you wanted complexity I could
give you complexity, machinery
far beyond grasp, extolling elucidation
and explication of profound, metaphysical
meaning, all that meaning attached
to everything life demands, but such is not
necessary, not warranted, when the snap
of a waistband joins up with all that
cosmic background radiation,
those baryonic acoustic oscillations
and chirruping gravitational waves,
all that wondrous movement
teaching all one ever needs to know.

JUSTIFIED

It had been years since
I'd gotten out of the Army.
No excuse then.

But someone had dumped
four bald tires on the lot line
shared with an incorrigible neighbor.

The city sent me a letter—
brusque, mean-spirited, informing me
of my violation: No tires allowed
for disposal and a fine if I did not
remove them.

I wanted the cops to fingerprint
the tires, find the miscreant
who had dumped them on my lawn.

I thought about dumping them
on that bureaucrat's lawn
at four o'clock in the morning. Something
for him to wake up to.

I thought of writing a letter,
but it is fruitless to argue with the city.

Nothing but futility and more aggravation
in that.

So I disguised them as garbage
and dumped them at the city dump,
the Disposal Center, as the city
prefers it to be called.

When someone left a grocery cart
on my curb, I called the store
that cart belonged to,
asked them to come and retrieve it.

They did not. Fearing another letter
from the city for this detritus left on my curb,
I called the grocer again,

And again, no response.

The cart sat there gleaming in the sun.
I imagine it carried someone's
belongings, and the homeless one
left it behind; perhaps an errant wheel
made the cart too hard to push.

Or, perhaps, someone in the neighborhood
with no resources for a car or a cab
pushed his groceries home
and left the cart on my curb.

Regardless,
I called again. Nothing. The next day
I took a crowbar and beat it to death,
bent every bit of wire on that cart,
beat it until it was nearly flat.

I took my reciprocating saw
and cut it into manageable sections,
loaded it up and took it to the dump.

I flung each piece as far as I could,
far as my anger took me.
I felt justified in my anger,
felt good about winning the war.

NEIGHBORHOOD WATCH

I

You would never imagine,
looking through the lattice
of late autumn trees—not a leaf
remaining, branches laced
like doilies—that the elderly woman
moving past curtains
of a window seldom opened
has stories to tell, lively tales
of children living far from home,
a husband she still talks to
though he's been gone for years,
a wheezing cat that sleeps
all day, all night, unfamiliar
to her lap now that the long
retreat has begun. Certainly, there are
calls, a scrap book, boxes,
more boxes, letters each writer
has even forgotten he'd written,
missives from old friends,
lovers during the war,
and art, her young boys'
drawings, everyone, everything, filled
with color, a palette of colors dreams make
and then forget, curtain closed
on the sun's muddy reflection.

II

Her children come back
only to make arrangements, talk to a lawyer,
want nothing of the contents,
house to be sold as is,
and a couple of neighbors from church
offer their time, volunteer
to clean out dozens of plastic bags
piled neatly in corners of the kitchen,
newspapers bundled in the basement,
cartons of cards, birthday greetings,
Christmas cards, many with crisp
ten or twenty-dollar bills,
a few uncashed checks
from banks no longer in existence,
and that one box of art: water colors,
oils, finger paintings, drawings
in chalk and crayon,
an entire box filled
with a mother's promise of joy,
her children filled with wonder,
every page a golden sun
and everywhere nothing but rainbow

NEW RECIPE

Approach love and cooking with reckless abandon
—Dalai Lama

This monastery soup looks good on the page,
something to try on a cool day:
I cut up leeks and carrots,
stalks of celery, add beans,
let them simmer in a large Le Creuset pot
heated on an old iron stove.
Steam rises when I add the rice,
condenses as the broth reaches
the heat of vaporization
though a taste confirms
its relative blandness,
perfect for a novitiate monk perhaps,
anyone forsaking earthly delight,
but I desire the whole of creation
so I push up the sleeves
of my robe, place the monk's hood
back on my shoulders and forage
through the cupboards.
It is like making love
to embrace perfumed herbs and spices
as love the first time
is like tea with extra bergamot
added, the pleasure increased
beyond limits of understanding,
the reaches of unquestioned faith.
I offer this bowl of simmering love,

steam rising in supplication,
my arms around your waist, your robe
falling with the scent of basil
and bay leaf to the kitchen floor.

LUNAR ECLIPSE

On the night of the eclipse
I am reminded there will be few
others scheduled in my life: to miss this
is to lose an image of understanding,
worldly and celestial at the same time.

Luminous and white, hanging large and heavy
above an undistinguishable horizon,
the moon appears visited by some dark-coated
stranger, as if standing in a brightly lit
doorway, a shoulder partially blocking
the light.

It all transfers slowly:
admittance, acceptance, the cold sparring
at night offering no resolution, no restoration.
This all takes time until finally
a black velvet hood covers the face
of the moon entirely, though a rim
of orange light remains, intransigent,
willful as ever, admitting that in all worlds
even the light must bend
but O so gracefully.

LOVE NOTE

That beautiful, wild caterpillar
Has venom in its spines—
Like that love of mine—
Colorful, sweet, and silken soft;
Yet, should I touch her in the wrong way,
Her sting will last for days.

LATE NIGHT AND A BLOODY ONE

I

Late night and a bloody one
at that. I hear the squeals
lying in bed reading of physics,
laws that govern the quantum
world, entanglement,
"spooky action at a distance."

I am, perhaps, a meliorist,
believing in perfectibility
long term, but for the present—

I know that owl has to eat to live,
but I prefer it not kill
outside my bedroom window.

Mercenaries killed in Syria.
Young Palestinians killed
as they throw rocks at soldiers
manning a checkpoint. "BLOODY BATTLE
IN AFGHANISTAN" reported early in Melville's
magnum opus. Twas ever thus,
same old, same old, and I hate clichés.

I want that weightless owl
to live, its world to flourish,
and whatever bloodied the ground
to find peace, unattainable in our time.

Something far distant changing it all
here,
in a new continuum.

II

Won't happen. I wake to the sound.

Somehow, *the Jew is still*
squatting on the windowsill.

And, an elderly, Asian woman,
American born,
is pummeled in the streets
for her role
in spreading the pandemic.

So little or nothing changes,
progress an illusion
in the way deceptive visual illusions—
the Necker Cube, the Müller-Lyer lines
of equal length—
are thought the work of the devil
if one voices susceptibility.

Piranesi, Escher, even susceptibility
becomes illusion whatever voice
calls out, isolate, intestate,
such benevolent annihilation
sure only of a bountiful sun singing,
paradise in an uncollected thought.

LAMENTATIONS OF THE BODY

Napoleon's penis
was sold at auction

Einstein's brain
sat in a jar for years

Thomas Hardy's heart
was left on a kitchen table
where it was eaten by a cat

Tycho Brahe lost his nose
in a duel with a drunken
mathematician, replaced it
with a silver and gold proboscis
held to his face each day with glue

And Mark Twain lamented
corpses floating to the surface
in Louisiana, dismembering
in the wash of rain,
the silted overflow of the river

So, nothing is held with reverence
nothing left intact,
ourselves dissembling
sometimes put on display
as curiosity, like a two-headed
calf at the county fair

And once, my own wife
despite my pleading
would not retrieve a chunk
of my thumb caught in a table saw,
thrown across the workshop
and buried in a pile of lumber,
roof shingles, architectural debris.

Nothing's sacred
I moan, offering another lamentation,
the itch of my opposable
thumb working in opposition
to everything deemed holy,
my own relics
unworthy of veneration,
left as a meal for scrounging mice.

DEAF HEAVEN

Plaintive cries and admonitions,
prayers and merry blasphemy,
all those O's and the O
strung out into a long, mournful
invidious sound that makes one
wish for silence, eternal silence
of the one damned with pain
excoriating heaven—a boundless
silence to be wished. Of course
heaven is deaf, the cacophony more
than any immortal can bear,
and I am joining their ranks—
can't hear a word on TV,
old movies just sludge in my ear,
hearing tests flat-lined
measuring the true pleasure
of heaven within my grasp—another
octave or two to lose and I'll be
home in a tireless world, tinnitus
like cosmic background radiation
and all else disappeared— the nightly news,
talk show banter, radio rants
and canned laughter, all that
insipid applause: I lean forward
cupping my ear, just that much closer
to God.

EXCURSUS

Flagellant lamplight
feudal colors
and a pastiche of sentiment

Is anybody ready for this?

Think of the change from
percolation to drip
avocado green to wasabi
containment to preemption

I like the way I've made adjustments,
slight tweaks in my sensibility
as the world changes
according to our needs

Today the last white dolphin died in China:
white, the absence of all color
or is it black?

I've forgotten over the years, there've been
so many alterations, so many shifts,
everything rushing away
faster than anyone can count

I have a machete from Rwanda,
it hangs over my fireplace like a fine print.

RESTORATION EPITAPH

My wife pensively notes
her tombstone should read:
Wife, Mother, Roofer—
to which I add, one early spring,
the moniker **Stone Cutter**
because it has since become
a yearly ritual to move stones,
a few that weigh nearly as much
as she does, to put them
in place—one over two, two
over one—the old prescription
followed by generations of men
who built stone walls, parapets,
wine cellars, cities, and castles
overlooking the world.

Those stones that don't have a place
ordained by their God-given shape
we cut, the diamond blade digging deep,
a fissure easily wedged
so the stone breaks apart
with a sharp blow,
stones perfectly shaped
to fit some space
in an elevated courtyard,
the walkways and garden walls
that define our yard, our lives,
the way we think of ourselves
even until death
splits us
like a stone.

REPAIRMAN LAMENTATIONS

Some jobs just have to be left undone,
left for others to complete—
a strange realization given
all the mornings he took phone calls
urging some repair be done quickly,
the world unable to mend itself, unable
to do its work without his.

But reflection too is a job,
and he thinks back on all the fallen porches,
leaking sinks, cracked window panes,
all needing attention that he gave
going from one job to another
ignoring the complaints of his wife,
the sullen looks of his son,
always a pleasant smile for each job.

Ten years from now that porch repaired
ten years ago will need repair again;
updated kitchens will undo his finest work,
and there'll be little left to show
for a long life fixing things,
keeping them alive awhile longer.

He sits at the kitchen table,
reflects on what goes wrong,
believes, in the end,
Things are pretty much left as they were
and smiles over coffee getting cold,
repeated rings of the phone ignored.

MILLINERY

My mother loved hats
and wore them faithfully
throughout her life
even when hats became
unfashionable, a vestige
of antiquated rules
and vanquished courtesy.

In old photographs, her hats
add more than a splash of splendor—
wild creations bedecked with plumage,
sculptured ones with mysterious veils
worn during the 40's, before and after the war,
but always hats in a grand style
only she could carry: the same hats
on someone else, her daughter, for example,
simply looked foolish, an affectation,
a comic absurdity, something of a laughable sport.

Wandering through antique stores
or second-hand clothing emporiums
I notice the hats, note how few
of the customers could wear them.
Sometimes, buried in a back room
on a long neglected shelf,
I find one she could have worn
and think of her sitting before her dressing
table on a night going out,
father proud as she put on her hat

before they walk out the door,
swirling in the perfumed
possibilities of pleasure and romance.

No one lives romantic in that sense
any longer—the kiss at the door
perfunctory, ambition a more bankable
virtue. I still remember my first kiss,
wonder about that woman's life
and how things turned out
though my own is more than I can manage.

Meditatively focused, I pick through
a shelf of hats, some still in elegant boxes
adorned with ribbons and bows.
I find one with white feathers—
resplendent, fiery-white plumes—
and remember the story, how
the Snowy Egret was hunted
unmercifully, almost to extinction,
feathers so desirable
they were worth many times their weight
in gold: I think of their long black beaks
melding to yellow-gold around the eye,
a small fish pinched, struggling in the beak
as the bird plundered along the salt marsh.

What was once desirable
is forbidden, illegal to possess, though every year
hunters kill them in their migratory haunts.
I wonder if my mother would have worn
a hat or evening dress sporting these feathers,
fashion and style trumping the loss.

Perhaps she would have celebrated their
fleeting beauty, knowing we are all
moving toward some indefinable
casting-off— love, beauty, everything turning
to a crystal residue in a cut glass bottle
that once held a favorite perfume
or an old memory buried in a careless pile
of veils and plumes.

EXCULPATION

How many obituaries have I missed,
missed with my own life
going on and on oblivious?
They meant something once:
a writer I loved— his lyrics
once resonated through every cell.
I taped his poems to my shower stall,
would memorize a few more lines
each day I washed, singing stanzas
as if they were the libretto
to a great Italian opera.

And the old girlfriends, their breasts
neatly fitting my hand, now lie flat
like overturned porcelain saucers,
those decorative, painted plates
my grandmother used to collect.
We gave them to Goodwill.
Perhaps I could look these women up; I could
find their stories, learn how much
I had missed.

I don't know what to do,
but I know I shouldn't do it.

And the cats buried in the back yard.
I've forgotten their names, the warmth
as they sat on my chest, searching my eyes
for some kindred spark of recognition.

Long, long ago I bought a camera from the Post Exchange
wanting preservation, the stamp of time
collected, and so I stood at evening
on a hotel tower, overlooking the temples,
the Asian palms listless below,
sensual city music coursing along the boulevards.

I clicked and clicked until I saw
so little I put the camera down,
knowing I should see and memorize
the scintillant lines of the city. Now I recall
the camera hung around my neck
thumping my chest
and the vista disappeared.

I took few photos (even of my wife, my child, my cats),
always believing their memory would stay with me,
the place, the experience, enhanced
by the process of living, not recording.
Now, with some early onset or another,
I have forgotten more than I have lived.

My neurologist probes and pokes with his pointed sticks,
barbless like fish hooks filed clean
for all those times I fished a sun-marked lake
far from anyone. The time was mine,
savored and relived as the glare rode down.

I want the doctor to stop. These knee-jerk reflexes
tell little; nerves once destroyed will not
grow back, pictures contained therein are lost,
and I laugh still at the nature program
recording an iguana swooped on by a Cooper's hawk,

its tail clasped in talons until torn loose,
and the iguana escapes, appendage to grow back
in a matter of days.

An enviable autotomy.

"Not like that in *my* life," I say to myself
(remarking on the wisdom of evolutionary process)
as the morning fades
and the coffee wears off.

And so, who is left? Who gone?
Whose words I will not be able to live by,
whose love I will not recall,
whose breast will not fit in my hand?

ENTOMOLOGICAL ASTRONOMY

Beetles navigate by light
from the Milky Way. I turn one over,
its legs flailing in the dark: righted, it follows
the path of eons, a river of efflorescing
stars. Yet I have learned galaxies recede
until eventually the sky eternally darkens,
and what then for beetles, for all of us,
the dark matter of our stories no longer
visible, our reach flailing like remembrance.

F=MA

When I was young
I was angry— perhaps
at the disposition of the world—
and contemplated the physics
of breaking glass with my fist,
the glass door to my bookcase
an arm's reach away.
I believed if I hit it hard enough
the glass would explode
before my hand and I'd receive
at best a bruised fist, all shards
blown forward with such force
nothing could hurt. I was partly
right—the glass shattered
explosively, knuckles bruised,
but the long deep cuts along the fleshy
inside of my thumb, my palm,
my wrist told another story no
equation could survive:
the blood ran hot and long
with what I learned—
still there in a calculus of scars.

THE WARMTH OF BLOOD

It is a singular scent
and taste, a reminder
of the promise of life,
an admonition to be careful,
and a sign that it's all right
to let go, never minding any consequence
because there isn't one: and how often
does anyone ever in this life
get to forsake everything and let go
leaving nothing behind in the gentle wake
of these years?

I can still feel the warm red sharing
as we made love, changing towel after
towel in an afternoon. I remember
blood washing down your thighs
as we showered, a taste of iron in the air—
all those years expecting the same
from one month to the next, except
during those months you carried our daughter,
and then the regular routine began again.
Until now, a month missed, an irregular
spotting the next, and the last time
measures its journey into the nothing
that lasts beyond everything—
that last test, a false positive,
signaling the uncertainty of change.

I rub your back from chill
to sweating chill.
It is like standing on shore
waving at old friends voyaging
to some place we've never been to,
promising to visit
but knowing we'll never see them again.

THE SACRED CHANGES

What was noble and venerable
becomes pedestrian,
a puerility.

May the Lord make his face
to shine upon you
becomes caricature,
a sacred satire.

Cartoon priests and infidels
make stylized signs of the cross
and followers follow.

Pretenders pretend to the will of God
yet know not a passage of scripture.

In the ranks of holy armies
bivouacked in the cradle of civilization,
even the lowliest soldier
recites the whole of gospel, psalm, and surah.

Any stumbling in the recitation
and his commander strikes his face.

Church leaders—ministers, priests, and nuns—
will not open their blood-red doors
arched to the heavens
when waters rise and wind rattles the glass.

In the most modern stained glass,
the followers of Jesus have buzz cuts.
Some wear T-shirts emblazoned
with the spirituous names of rock groups
boasting the years and cities of their tours.

The Yazidis say peace
comes only with guns and money.

We say guns and a good butter substitute
are promised and desirous.

Assuredly, one can always have both:
wealth *and* decency; The Beatitudes
and the plucking of an eye.

I keep an old octagonal barreled .22
in the recesses of an unlit closet.
My Confirmation Bible is on the shelf.
I don't recycle, any longer, my aluminum cans.

I gave up butter months ago.

THE GOSPEL OF PHILIP

It is said
that
one hundred years
from now
no one
will care
who you made love to

whether
faithful wife,
clandestine lover
someone who indulges every
fanciful delectation
a tropical fulfillment
as if love were the lively riches
most desired

a woman perhaps met
by the sea on a summer night:
you return to the hotel
late and she waiting,
leaning back
against the portico

A fondling wind off the sea
frolics in her hair

She is bold perhaps
because of the sea,

its warmth the breeze
she feels on her lips.

She asks you
not to retire
to stay
and talk awhile
have a drink
to enhance the conversation

It is too early to go in
and the breeze is so warm

You say the break
between sea and sand
night sky and water
is enough an intoxicant
like leaves
embracing the dark
in their slow dance
trees clinging like lovers
to the sky

And she says No
it is time for lights and music
and the thrill of a strong liqueur
to hold her in its sway

So you go with her
and the pleasure
carries the sweet scent
of the sea the rapture

of the movement
its cadence and rhythm

And all night long
you play through every
earthly delight
and it stays with you
a hundred years
or more
long after anything
not even the world
matters

HUMAN TERRAIN

— And in an instant, suddenly, you will be visited . . . with thunder and with earthquake and great noise, with whirlwind and tempest, and the flame of a devouring fire. Isaiah 28:6

The proper translation of Solomon's
epiphany isn't *All is vanity* though
such is found everywhere—
belief in hegemony among nations,
the necessity of imposing one's hegemonic will:
consider my neighbor manicuring his lawn,
a smell of fertilizer, herbicide,
permeating my living room as it wafts through
the window. I can't concentrate
even on the silliest TV; I think of stiff,
impregnated uniforms harder than starch,
bulwark against VX, GB, HD, and laugh
wishing I had my old protective mask.
My neighbor bends over, stiffly, slowly,
his lawn groomed to an all-conforming vanity,
and presses a multitude of small signs
into the grass, signs required by law
warning, **Danger! Herbicide & Pesticide**
Application: Do Not Walk or Play
on the Lawn. No, the proper translation
I'm told, explained by a studious seminarian
who almost took his vows but quit
choosing a secular life instead,
reads *All is pfff*, a sound like the last breath

of air pressed from a bicycle tube
as it's compressed when removed from the rim,
the sound of everything, one time or another,
like the theory of everything, this the sound
of the ephemeral, everything vanishing, *pfff*,
the sound we've all heard
taking our breath away, present always,
background noise to the cosmos as evidenced
when the Religious Program Specialist—
what we used to call a Chaplain's Assistant—
tells me of being on patrol, long hours
penetrating deep through stone portals,

along rock ledges, landscape of scarf and scree
treacherous as any promise made
by faithful and infidel alike. A soldier
stops, kneels and *pfff*, gone, vanished,
all ears ringing in the silent rain
of dust, blood dry as rock and sand,
as a pebble placed in one's dry, cottony mouth
to cure a desiccated tongue
to allow speech but there is none
all vanished in the heat of vaporization,
and he saw his Christian friend
disappear, an IED that could slash
and gut a Humvee,
turned just at that moment
to see him kneel and *pfff*
nothing left because all is vanity
and what stays is the nothing that is there
and is not there; his face recedes, his name,
not even a replacement because time is short

and the mission, the prayer, *pfff,*
an image not an image staying
and staying because where else the scripture
that explains *pfff . . . pfff . . . pfff.*

HONORED DUST

From gardens and an old orchard
at the back of her house—painted yellow
in her youth—a greenhouse at the side,
wends a path just wide enough
for *two in love*, and on this warm,
bee-laden afternoon in Amherst
we circumnavigate the lawns,
trek to her brother's and Susan's house
and on return we visit her drawings—
vassal crocuses, violets, cypripedium—
walk to the room at the top of the stairs
that holds her dress,
and I stand next to this dress,
study fascicles stitched together—
a gathering of poems—recall
how a friend stopped by, at night,
took a photograph of the Dickinson house,
found a presence in her writing room
when the film developed, a matter
of bad photography one might say
by way of explication, a trick
of the light, the shadow of evening,
but her presence fills that dress, still,
as I look over her shoulder,
her figure diminutive, like her poems,
holding all circumference of this world.

A LEGAL ARGUMENT

On the trail,
carnage,
strips of fur and flesh,
dollops of blood
the size of small change.
My eye tracks
along the brush,
turns to a patch of grass
where a hawk
stares me down,
pulls at the rabbit's
meat, tears it
into strips
with his scimitar
beak.
I stop but a few
feet away from
his killing field,
his eyes
lit with defiance
daring me
to come closer,
to just try
to steal
some of his kill.
I read his eyes,
backtrack slowly
knowing what's mine,
what's lawfully his.

A COLD NIP

A cold nip in the air as if a dog
bites a child in play that isn't play,
first sweatshirt of the season,
a faint drizzle, and a few geese
flying low give a boisterous,
accusatory honk of good bye—
Yes, I think, *you're right;*
time to get out of here.

The neighbor's wife is dying;
he says he'll leave after her death;
nothing holds him here any longer.
Nothing holds anyone here any longer
if one reads the daily news:
IED's, suicide bombers, Tamil Tigers
fighting a battle they always lose.

On the sports page always an ad
for a Gentleman's Club near the airport;
women take off their clothes for men just
traveling through. They aren't allowed to touch—
everything unobtainable, a great tease at a great cost,
as always a pleasure doing business. No matter the cost
we stay. A year later the neighbor
is still here; he has nowhere else to go. He yells *Stay!*
to his dog when the mailman approaches.
Even most of the geese fly back.

ACQUISITION

A child plays in the library dust

even the windows have a heavy film

leaded glass makes landscapes
playful in the light

an Expressionist painting
seems out of place in a room
filled with Old Masters,
their solid reproductions

the child loves this room,
walls lined with books,
that heavy desk, that heavy pen

the books are heavy and solid
as well, the weight of time
such that the boy is curious,
so much withheld

there is a wish worth risking

a locked bookcase holds up a wall
near a window studious with its light

each book seems a lock unto itself
and the child traces his finger
in the dust on the bookcase,

on a world where promises
break from their locks

risking everything

WHAT IT'S LIKE

It is like going to summer camp
and missing your family
or making the mistake of making a friend
who wet his mattress each night,
and each day that mattress is put out
in the sun in front of your tent,
and you are embarrassed he is your friend
because everyone makes fun of him,
even the counselors, especially the counselors,
and you want to join in, to have a family
for two weeks, although you wish they'd all
drown in the lake like your friend
who, they said, probably wet the lake bed
as he went under.

YELLOW

(after the surgical removal of cataracts
from a man blind since birth)

Yellow, its first perception, caused vomiting
and a dizzy feeling in his head; citrines swirled
and rippled in shallow depths of hue like currents
of the sea—a sea of color crashing on his brain:
yet gradually, as days passed, the shadows
of yellow stayed like the mend of a broken bone.
Surfaces flecked with paint and litter blown
down city streets through oily spills of tar
caused such depression that he longed to have
his cloudy vision back—to make his milky eyes return
imaginative perfection and flowers that never paled or fell.

Just so, the objects around him lost the aura of their trust—
stairs seemed so much higher, tables nearer
and projecting harm; his cat's teeth seemed so cruel
in contrast to her warming touch of fur.
And other things, quite simply, were unrecognizable
until he held them in his hands—a spoon, a glass,
each looked as if it might have been some other thing
until his fingers closed around it, until the hardness,
the texture, the slippery shape gave evidence
and the recognizable pleasure of knowing.

Inside each visionary cell resides a template
of some external thing, and when the image is disturbed,
displaced, a pitted stone remains: but like some undiscovered
particle that makes the world make sense,

a human substance is transformed, and images are born
beyond each sense and feigned recognizance.

He crossed the street with trepidation
now that he could see the cars,
and soon refused to leave his room
or look out of the filmy window glass
on those who believe in dreamy visions of their lives—
behave as though these visions are the same for all.
Illumined objects and ideas appeared as monumental
relics of despair, and thoughts conceived in tactile ways
gave way to visions of repair. He dreamed of being deaf,
of having ears restored to symphonies of light.
He felt that words must seem like knives
cutting at each cell and braved evisceration
with each attendant appellation:
a rush of blood exploded in his brain
as swirling syllables of light echoed into meaning
and perceptible decree. He sensed how sounds of images,
like light, were particles and waves—still pure sensation
yet the warming radiation passed straight through.

He counted oranges with his hands and counted days the same—
the roughness disappeared: all color and its light,
like some nocturnal beast, crept back
into a silver prism of its years. Fluorescent bulbs burned out
were not replaced; the shades stayed drawn
until one night, beneath the changing pictures
of the sky, he pressed his palms against his eyes
and prayed that he might see
some hueless tint, some vitreous orpiment,
some colors other than the dingy rainbows of this world.

WIFE IN WINTER

I can't number the number of winters,
all the rages of snow and blind wind, drifts
piled behind our house, waves of frozen snow
that mimic Japanese prints of a roiling sea;
even Shackleton would have toiled
to reach the garage: shovels, snow blower,
ice breaker, buried in a mausoleum of white.
A rink of frozen sleet engenders deceit,
lies under the snow from a hard rain
pelting our coats with buckshot
the day before; I watch her put on the same coat
worn season after season, the same scarf
and boots, even her gloves have seen a better
year. At the bottom of the drive, she lifts
a shovelful of snow onto a pile above her head—
I'm sorry and feel sad for the years, the yelling
about how to lift the shovel full of snow
with her legs, not her arms, to save her back
as she clears the stairs, the route
to the mailbox; she still does it her own way,
the way I suppose of winter, wearing us down:
a new coat would mean nothing,
and I can't promise the sun.

AS SIMPLE AS THAT

My daughter sends me
a photograph of her cat, her lone cat,
lying on her bed next to two other
cats, her boyfriend's cats
that have just moved in.

They seem to like being together,
no turmoil over the turf,
no petty jealousies
evinced as they lie there, resting
in a cat's repose.

I think of times lying next to my wife,
just lying there, no movement,
merely an occasional touch,
a hand trailing lightly
along the arm, the shoulder.

It is as if we were cats;
nothing profound escapes our lips,
nothing of importance
to communicate, to fill the silence.

What is profound is the silence,
the touch, the recognition
that this space is filled,
that words are an unnecessary encumbrance
like an additional blanket
when we are already warmed enough.

A TROPICAL PHILOSIPHY

What is less or more than a touch?
— Walt Whitman

A venomous millipede crosses my path
and her hand grabs my arm
pulling me back: a small cry
and a stern warning cut through
shimmering depths of sun.
Strange how I remember the touch
of her hand, really a warning in itself,
how my chest draws in a breath
deeper than any usual respiration
with this remembrance: and she would
take so many breaths away,
mine and others, an extraordinary power
which in the wrong hands makes waste
and despair of everything.

Untouchable.
Practiced as an art. What of it?
But why not? An urbanologist's walk
through major cities, ancient and modern,
records the disconnect, the separation, a disdain
for the presence, the closeness of others;
the architecture closing down, excluding
the most modest of contact: forbidding white walls,
temples and tombs, cool to the hand.
Yet within it all the need, the blessing

of the hand touching another, even or
especially as warning though I'd rather
have the fatal sting than any soft
remembrance.

CYCLO

Lost in Hanoi late, endless streets unmarked
and few lights, I've strayed far
from the lakes, and it's so dark
I can't read my hotel map. My chest
feels heavy, landmarks, directions,
skewed. And then the quick release:
I don't care if I find my way back;
I'll never again be in this place
moving like this through the Annamese dark,
men dragging from doorways
the daily trash, getting ready
for the next day's work. If there is loss
I live for it as recompense,
and I'm almost sorry a cyclo
stops, knowing with certainty
I must be lost. He offers me a ride
back to the hotel, a long way back,
and I wouldn't have gotten there on my own
until long past dawn if I hadn't
given in, accepting some small grace
this world still has to offer.

COVERING OLD GROUND

We've gone over this a thousand times
as tall grass beckons in the wind
pine sap glistens on the peeling bark

It's part of the blood by now
the stream slows and parts
breaks around the carcass of a doe
shot last season

But if I've learned anything
it's nothing more than I already knew
the learning of a child
the years don't bring that much
that's useful or good
and I was smarter then
I could think anything and live

I said, I can make this bet and win
every time—
in twenty years we'll meet right here
and argue the same old things
the world will be the same:
drugs and politics, the war and revolution,
the usefulness of art
salvaging that inability
to do anything that matters or works,
our best just barely gets us by

Worn down like an old coin,
faces hard to recognize
we remember promises, the old gifts
and we return to find them
flung along the ground like stale bread
thrown out to colorless birds in the backyard

The sky runs deep, the air cold
across the common ground:
we have unfailing lies to keep us warm

STILL LIFE: LAMENTATIONS OF THE NUDE

I tell you the street was narrow,
so narrow I could see everything
in the townhouse across from mine,
her window open in the summer heat

and it was evening as she stepped
from the bath, stood there
drying her hair with a towel,
drops glistening, beaded on her shoulders

and then maybe I moved,
or she looked up
and saw me standing there
across the way watching:
she froze, thinking perhaps
I'd detect any movement, or perhaps
she was embarrassed
standing there nude,
a stranger watching.

She walked into the shadows
of another room, her bedroom most likely
where she dressed, covered her lovely array
of earthly delights; perhaps she blushed
at their revelation.

Weeks later, the height of August,
city hot as a torch

she moved her bed near the window
and one night lay there nude
except for a black ribbon,
an ivory cameo, around her throat.
She slept, the lamp on her nightstand lit

and I watched her all night long—
too humid to sleep, to think, to dream:
she must have known, but the heat,
the stale city air, overcame any inhibition
or perhaps she knew pleasure doesn't last,
and you might as well give or

take as much as you can, as much
as you have, before everything melts,
before those eidetic images
of what matters most
curl and char in the white heat
leaving your loss naked and exposed,
a breath of ash swirling in your lungs.

THE NATURAL WORLD

There is a brooding loveliness in this swamp,
patterned shadow lying quietly
on the brackish water, trees flourishing
half-submerged, a loveliness as eternal
as men finding faith among the faithless.
My old cedar canoe is at rest,
and the water is so still, the odor
of health. It is only an imagination
which perturbs the depths, discovery
of cells disruptive, lymph nodes
swollen like the belly of a snake
after a good and nourishing kill; for years
the prostate grows, an additional piss
in the night and then more until
there is no more. The surface breaks,
and something sinks beneath: predator
or prey, it makes so little difference.
Always, something is eaten alive.

REMEMBRANCE OF THINGS SAID

Proust's *Madeleine* first was *toast,*
so when I say, "You're toast, this whole
relationship is toast!" in the heat of an exchange,
accusations bouncing off the hard surfaces
of our lives, the hard, hard heads we both live with,
the stone silences we use as barricades
and broadsides, the granite countertop
providing an exclamation point
for my slammed down mug of tea,
think only this: toast
was really cake, soft, delectable,
a sugary confection offering
the sublime—our after words entwining
should be as sweet.

REJECTION

I come at the gatekeeper
from a different direction
and still I may not enter.
Password forgotten or changed,
required totem still buried
in some ancient archaeological dig,
there is no magic key to this kingdom
so I return, admonished, scolded,
to work at this another way,
surreptitious, sneaky, knowing
it's the only way I'll ever get inside;
I'll learn something else, pretend
I'm someone else or else
I'll pay hell to have me there.
Or not. Wishes and bona fides
obtain. Why not sit on the back porch
and watch my cats slink low to the ground
hunting insects flittering out of reach? Why not
imagine the gate already opened
and me inside exactly where I am,
content as the cat that's given up,
rolling happily in the sun,
butterflies and honey bees just slightly
beyond my reach, Nirvana unobtainable,
a sweet acceptance always in my hands.

SUSPENSION OF BELIEF

It is a slow morning
I wake to

I sing a song to myself,
the world beyond hearing range
and begin the routine
of daily living

It is a constant
as formidable as any
constant in the realm
of mathematics or physics

As inviolable as Avogadro's number
or Euler's **e**
or the speed of light in a vacuum

But wait—this is a strange morning:
light slows, 38 mph,
as it travels through a Bose-Einstein condensate

And I know, as cold as it might be outside,
I am nowhere near the temp
of that condensate

But traffic noise has abated
streets soundless, and wind
through the trees dropping

dollops of last night's rain
has kept those drops in mid-air

It will take years before they fall
to the ground

As if gravity failed
suspended for a time

Remember that shock of realization—
all synapses firing at once—
when told that space can travel
faster than the speed of light,
that the visible universe
is only part of what is known

Still, a bumblebee hovers an inch
from the dahlia potted on the porch
and a scarlet tanager
will never reach the feeder

This day, this unusual day,
moves so slowly
I can do nothing, as if living
in a still photograph,
a photo you would never see
in this slowness, even if I placed it
carefully in your hand.

REFLECTION

A bombed-out church in Rouen
has been turned into a small park.
A few old men sit on a bench
smoking, a couple of older lovers
appear disinterested in each other
as if their lives have broken
like the choirs of this ruined church,
not quite gone, but left wanting.
The church garden lives in neglect,
and there is some missing history
on the commemorative plaque:
no mention of congregants
desiring solace and calm
who came here to worship,
kneeling in prayer before
the bombs fell, so much in their world
blown out like these heavy stone walls,
like so many candles on the altar.

STRATEGY

Today I needed to touch
something to give this day
a personal credibility
it had been in danger of losing.

I misplaced yesterday
thinking it was today, virtue
filtering through the trees
like sunlight. I reach out

to touch a tree, pick up a small stone
fallen from the garden wall,
everything feeling better, my hand
pressing against the bark,
pressed hard around the stone.

SO MANY YEARS AGO

So many years ago
we stood on the back porch,
looked out across the barren drive,
imagined old, red brick
laid all the way from the house
to a Victorian flower bed
luxuriantly planted in front of
the old stone wall,
and this year we rebuilt
that wall, laid bricks
in an interwoven pattern
that takes the eye
to an excavated planting bed,
eight yards of stone and clay removed—
soil that couldn't grow weeds—
and eight yards of rich black soil
heaped there in its stead,
and then you planted— fall
being unseasonably warm—
several hundred bulbs:
so now we wait—the first flurries
will come tonight, winter soon
to follow, and we will wonder
as the earth grows cold
of crocus, tulip, daffodil, and lily.
It's been a long wait
through the flowering of our lives
our house gutted and restored,
a legacy of love and marriage

that's endured like this old frame house
here since the end of our nation's
Civil War—what else is there
but the promise of color
the generation and regeneration of love
as we age with each spin of the earth:
the bulbs take root even as we stand again
on the old back porch, my arm
around your waist, awaiting winter,
its strong hold, its love of color,
its certain passing.

PERFECTION OF THE LIFE OR OF THE WORK

In the middle of a chilly night
my grandfather walked down the stairs—
his slippers clopping, his pajamas worn thin—
unlocked the front door and shuffled
down the block, a dim street lamp
guiding his footsteps. Cops stopped,
asked him the usual questions: name,
where he was going, where he lived.

He said he was going to work
as he had for so many lifetimes,
repeating the same ritual
as if taking communion every day
of his life. Maybe it is the work
that keeps us going, the work
never ending, always something to do,
rest saved for another life
beyond the halo of a street lamp.

FUBAR

As a species we can abbreviate
anything. I do so because of my age—
so little time left to spell it all out.
The Colonel says to the civilians,
"You must be puzzled by all the acronyms."
TPFDL, STRAC, AMRAAM, SIPRNET.
They don't respond, nodding silently
in the most barren reaches of their minds,
making up phrases to fit the initials. LSMFT.
Think of each letter as a nematocyst,
a stinging alphabet, a rebuke
to monographs and intensive study. TLDR.
One can't learn it all so why bother
learning anything at all: absorb the initials
until whatever they stand for
dissipates like morning fog upon the hills
or caffeine wearing off as the morning wends.
So now what? LQTM. A series of disconnected
episodes, a bland recognition of more repetition?
FFS: RTFM. Every day blends into every other
until they are one. Every sermon
pleads the same. So many go gluten free
unable to memorize FODMAPS. My doctor
is scheduled to read my DNA. I am asked to initial
here and here. IRL the long story goes unread;
I can make it up as I go along.

ARIEL

She followed me home, a young stray
I picked up on my nightly
rounds in Philadelphia,
packets of moist cat food
in my pockets. Every night
the same cats came out
from under porches,
the back alleys of row houses,
the campus where students
left them to forage on their own
after classes ended for the year.
Glossy black, golden eyes, and pregnant
she seemed listless
as if the spirit were lifted
from her knowledge of the world
and she lay with me in the dark
curled against my legs
for warmth. I called the vet
the next day but he was gone
for the weekend. On Sunday
she died, kittens still warm
in her belly; a knife lay
on the kitchen counter,
sharp enough to filet
a fish, cut through
shark skin if need be
or serve as a heart
surgeon's scalpel.
I held it in my hand,

tested its sharpness
on my thumb, then tossed it
into the sink. I buried
her that night in a park
under a tree, knelt down
for the first time in years,
knees damp from the cooling grass
felt the chilling sickle of moon
so sharp it could slice
through anything
I had to pray for.

ARRIVALS

Cold air knocks at the window
as if a welcome guest, visitor
from long ago and yet
it has been but a year
counting the months
like coins

We count everything

There is a ledger for everything

I can't remember
how to differentiate
ordinal
from cardinal numbers

I know the difference is important

Like the difference between one infinity
and another

They are not the same

And this is not the same winter
as last

Not the same breath on cold glass

The difference is in the coins
clinking into my hands

COGNITION TEST

What do a fence and an anchor
have in common?
I sit there, as usual, perplexed
by the workings of the universe.
She repeats the question.
I say they both occupy space.
They are both constructed by humans,
not by alien life forms surreptitiously
inhabiting North America.
They will both disappear
when our planet goes up in flames
a billion years from now,
a time long before our species
gains much common sense.
I say Noah dropped anchor
during the flood so he wouldn't sail
to New Jersey. I say he built a fence
around that anchor as the waters receded
to keep out the creatures let loose
who would eat the greens in his garden.
She looks at me, convinced of my cognitive
decline. I tell her the anchor is in Kansas;
there is a fence around it still.
This all makes sense in Kansas, I say.
You should visit; take a long
vacation after this test is over.

ANY ANTIQUE STORE ON MAIN

Whole families, great legacies, can be bought here
boxes of photos, complete family histories
as if the past, as if our ancestors
were as disposable as our lighters and pens.
The dealer jokes, says you can change
your family tree, get rid of relatives
you don't like, replace jailed cousins
with respectable rich uncles,
a fiction worthy of ourselves.
The photos are silent and grim
as they look at us from the bottom
of a shoebox. We thumb through,
one life after another, catch a likeness
we remember. The dealer leaves us
to our culling, the photos reticent,
some undecipherable as we search through,
wondering, questioning where a particular shot
was taken: On a front porch, a woman
sits in a rocking chair, a child on her lap:
the white frame house sits solitary
on the prairie, nothing but farmland
stretching behind. We marvel at the beauty
passed from mother to daughter, from
daughter to granddaughter, a lively spirit
in their eyes passed down again and again
in a sequence of photos capturing their lives.
We sort through one story after another
until the photos speak, hearing our rootless

cry taking us back. “Talk to us,” they say,
“Let us finish the story. There was so much
left unsaid. Help us remember.
Take us home.”

A WALK HOME FROM SCHOOL

Still winter, but the sun burned
ice on a crooked sidewalk
(one slab raised above another
by burgeoning tree roots)
burned to a water gazer's inviting puddle,
and I joyfully ran through it splashing,
but the uneven slabs tripped me
and I fell, wetting my pants, my mittens,
my jacket, in the ice-cold water.

My mother was displeased
but dutifully washed my cold, wet clothes,
and I wore them again the next day.

But again the sun shone
and the same puddle, an invitation,
a dare perhaps, and I took it
believing experience would get me through,
reasoning I could not be outsmarted
by a simple puddle of water.

And again I tripped
and again the displeasure,
a mild scold though accepting
of what young boys do
followed by the eternal repetition,
her obedient washing and ironing
of the same clothes washed and ironed
the day before.

I should have learned something:
that I could easily be defeated,
that arrogance meeting the natural world
would be fraught with error,
tribulations for a lifetime.

No such luck. No such understanding.
What came of this, so many years later,
was the motherly patience shown,
the immeasurable bond
between parent and child.

So when my daughter puddle-jumped crazily
into playground canyons and crevasses
covered with thin sheets of winter ice
reveling in the explosions of ice water,
the sound of crackling ice,
I let her, and without her mother knowing,
placed her wet snow suit and mittens
her saturated socks and scarf,
into the warmth of the dryer.

When I complained to my mother
of her granddaughter's rambunctious
nature, her inquisitiveness,
her penchant for trouble, her daily experiments
(once she climbed a nine foot pole
to grab a basketball rim, hanging so precariously
her mother never went to the playground with her again),
my mother responded with karmic understanding,
recognizing the generational payback, the pleasures
amidst all the pitfalls, saying, "*You* got you,"
a wondrous smile across her face. "What you have there,

in your beautiful daughter,
just another incarnation of you."

A MAN WE KNEW

But mildly famous in some quarters,
a writer, veteran of our forgotten war,
it is surprising to find a small piece buried
in a back page of the daily news—
a simple admission of disruption.

If you were there you saw a man walk quickly,
aberrantly, down this crowded street;
he bumps into the free flow of pedestrians
reminding one of particles bombarded in a physics lab.
Recollect the mouse trap fission experiment,
the chain reaction that results when a single ball
is dropped on a field of unsprung mouse traps,
each holding a stationary ball, and when that single ball
descends and strikes a ball in a trap,
all the traps snap shut unleashing a fury,
a torrential cascade of other balls
bouncing wickedly against each other;
the pounding escalates as wires snap, traps jump
and the balls collide.

Isn't that entropically true
of everything ever known or valued:
cherishing a simple moment, a silly object
(a class ring, a letter or gleaming trophy
in a sport no one cares about,
the license plate of a first car,
a medal won in the war)

loss compounding loss, pleasure ascending
until it dissipates and leaves one wanting.

So much given, expended on so little.

And so few wondered why he fell,
cleaving a small space on our city streets.

And why not? Why not stumble and yell
profane assessments of the world at large,
assume a wild posture, human traffic offended
by such violation of the social norm?

Yet, may this not be more honest,
more acutely human than acceptance,
that sycophantic obedience that sickens
until knees crack upon the pavement—
supplicants all, believers to the end,
our congregation insistent to go home.

THE FAMILY CAR

In northern Wisconsin—
lake country and pine woods—
junkyards are not surrounded by fence,
no graffiti panorama
obscuring the wrecks:
here cars line up
on hillsides in long rows,
cars from decades ago
still used for parts.

A blue '52 Dodge
catches in the sun
as I drive by; its chrome
still shines, its large fenders
curve and flow above the highway.

I pull in, drive up the hill
past the gate, check in,
walk out into that field of cars,
all the years laid out
like a family album:
there's a '56 Buick, its grille
still grinning, a '59 Plymouth,
fins ready to fly.

The blue has faded on the Dodge,
its chrome rough with corrosion,
years left to the elements.
I run my hand along the fender,

lift up the hood, close it, open the door
and crawl behind the wheel.

We were so little then
mom removed handles
from the car's back windows
so we couldn't roll them down and lean out,
or put our hands into the dark summer night
as we sat at the edge of the county dump
to watch brown bear browse and forage
through piles of refuse: once a foolish man
got out of his car to feed them
popcorn—he nearly lost his arm.

All those vacations at the lake,
that first glittering glimpse
as the car turned through the pines,
the long trek to Mt. Rushmore,
buffalo burgers, corn husk dolls,
the trips to school and a crew cut,
custard stands on a warm summer night,
drive-in movies where we always
fell asleep before the film began,
and the drive to great grandmother's
funeral, past corn fields filled
with light.

All those car games played
to pass the miles, radio static
as we rolled down a hill
reading Burma Shave poems—
and those Sunday drives
when my grandfather told

of what the land was like
before we were born—
farms extending for miles
where subdivisions now stand,
silos torn down, modern steeples
pinned against the sky.

I lean back behind the wheel,
look in the rear view mirror,
backseat still plush with childhood,
all of life glowing ahead
like a lighted ornament
on the hood.

WARRIOR'S LAMENT

So the war ended and the wreckage
burned to ash, hardened with cold, air viscous
and damp with gray rain, slop-wash flooding the streets
and then the mopping up, everyone grateful

Except those who stumbled through the ruins
of one day after another, graceless, nameless
after all they'd been through—a thankless lot,
the living, landmarks crumbling at their touch,

Char deep in their lungs, a taste of what
forever brings when nothing is its due—
just a test of what is false and true,
and yet one other wandered out

Upon this map, streets creased and folded
stopping at the maze of options, landscape littered
with impassable debris. He looked hard, looked far ahead,
foresaw a dark time filled with everlasting peace

He thought of time behind a desk,
a wife smiling on his return from work,
of puttering in the garage, lawn work, kicking
the mower when it wouldn't start,

All things considered as eventful
in that life men do aspire to, making
things that work, that build, that pass the time
until puttering is all that's left—

Easy yet unforgiving time. He shuddered,
tossed a ream of paper in the trash, looked out
his office window on the street below, knew no peace
lasts, and smiled, and waited for the hour to pass

WINTER IN BRUSSELS

Cold night in Brussels
and after a long walk
through the old city
I sit in a café,
order a simple dinner
and stare at postcards
pinned to the wall—
photographs of elsewhere,
notes from another country
where the sun is warm
the beaches bare, except
a few women topless
lying on the sand—
another of a woman walking,
a wrap around her waist,
decorously shading her eyes
averting our glance,
her feet leaving tracks
like shorebirds in the sand—
this must be some other world,
some other life, where a touch,
a simple kiss, burns like hot sand,
where imagination
has reached its limit,
where the mind
sings like water.

THE CARPENTER'S LAMENT

A woman's shoe, circa 1870,
and the curve of her calf
rising out of that shoe
but no more of her leg
are drawn on the sheathing—
wide, smooth boards beneath
worn cedar clapboards—drawn by a carpenter
who had thoughts and desires other than
just crafting this old Victorian,
a venerable but neglected Queen Anne:
gingerbread, fretwork, rotting beneath
so many layers of paint, milk paint,
lead based paint, modern oil and latex,
paints of so many colors, most
not appropriate to the age;
so underneath everything is something
to be discovered—original colors,
drawings pornographic to the times,
the high button shoe,
that woman's leg, its delicate
and perfect contours, the fleshy curve
of the calf, a synecdoche of pleasure
outlasting even my imagination
as I wonder about her knee
and how much further I might go,
just a kiss of the knee and how much longer
it might take to unlace that shoe,
the hook fumbled in my hand
as I arrest the curve that outlasts

generations of carpenters and lovers,
our aesthetic meditations
lost in the long unlacing,
that lifting of the skirt above her knee.

ALL THE WEALTH AND SPLENDOR

I make my morning rounds,
the daily circuit, pick up
candy wrappers, a cat's eye
marble, a child's homework
blown across the grass.

A dead woodpecker lies beside the house.

I kneel, as much in contemplation
as in wonder at the beauty of it all,
the white and black stilled to
a point of meditation. Emerson said
there is beauty even in a corpse,
and always, I said, the beauty was
in living, and thus my life, this morning,
these rounds, curtailed by a dash
of red, plumage fanciful, panache
that sings even in death, and what else
will fall, the grace of the sky gone wild?

THE BLOUSE

She brings home a new blouse,
like all her other blouses in a way,
like one day, one life, one of everything
is like another,
and the differences are small
but this print is simple and evocative,
fabric smooth and delicate
and when she tries it on
it looks so good, so luscious
I want to save it for another time
and take it off as quickly as I can.

A MOST UNLITERARY PARABLE

My friend who is one fucked-up
VN vet goes to his shrink
every other week. He tells jokes—
some almost funny— until his allotted time
runs out and the next psycho takes his place.

I tell this to my psychologist,
ask her what she makes of it,
all those jokes, the banter, nothing
ever confronted or changed. She says,
"We're not here to talk about him;
we're here to talk about you,"
to which I reply, "Isn't what I'm telling you
the same thing, places we cannot go?"

She has no answer to that—brutal
self-assessment that it is. It is like
a high-priced automobile, all those
technological systems, avoidance software
preventing any tailgating, any collision
front or rear, no unsafe lane changes.

. . .

A brutish anger wakes the day.
No one behaved well over night
and the news records our misbehavior
spread across the globe.

This is not a legitimate piece of writing;
it doesn't pass the smell test,
bullshit detector on the blink.
It passes the same, like those therapeutic sessions,
nothing accomplished, nothing worked
as she says, "to get me where I want to be."

I don't want to be *here* for certain.
I've read the DSM, the CFR,
and very little there. One evening long ago I fed
a stray cat through a broken window.
It visited my third floor apartment
wary and hungry as any stranger
in an unforgiving place. A triangle
of broken glass sliced open my arm
when I drew it back; the stray fed

to its contentment. Blood ran down my arm,
dripping past my wrist, my fingers shaking
with an electric sting. I stanched the blood,
my bath towel crimson, a beautiful crimson,
but I thought the need to sew this vacant space together,
though I'm not left-handed, nor ambidextrous.
Reluctantly I ventured out, to the nearest ER,
and the ER nurse, unwrapping my towel,
winced—not a good sign.

My arm sewn up after a long wait.
I walked back to my apartment,
back to lie down and reflect:
The social contract, reciprocal
at its core, expectations and obligations,
duties and responsibilities

shared each to each. Some things
require another's assistance,
some things need to be fed in the dark.

AN ECONOMY OF CHARACTERS

My parents subscribed
to the local newspaper,
gossip mainly, of interest
only to one's neighbors, friends,
people met on the rounds
of one's daily life, a life I never
wanted, would do anything to escape,
and they would read the obituaries,
recognizing old names, schoolmates,
distant relatives, childhood chums
passed out of their lives
decades and decades before,
and that was news,
a record of one's life, unchanging,
unceasing, unparalleled except
in the way parallel lives approach
the vanishing point and converge
in a clipping, cut and stored in a drawer,
never to be read again.

AMNESTY

When this is over
there will be so little to say,
so very little reason to say it,
the pure present ungraspable,
the indefatigable past within;
without, a primordial history obtains:
metals in our bodies build from stellar
explosions unfathomably distant
in deep time, and speech born of this
as well, language, our singular creation,
bears witness, yet its grand misuse
defines our evolutionary course.

Back then, the world, that foolish war,
pressed us apart, all of us
afraid to accept this covenant
and embrace a vow of simple speech
eloquent in its brevity
and the long spaces between.

Remember the language
of those first teenage dates
when words came thick as oily sludge
draining from a worn-out, over-heated
Chevy V-8, your date wordlessly nervous
as well, the dead-air space between you
empty, and your jokes fell flat. But now,
now, silence is treasured and desirable.

It is a gravid, febrile voice that signs
these messages; I need ignore this world—
let schoolchildren walk to playgrounds
in twos and threes, learning to sing
barefaced conceits. We learned to sing
When Johnny Comes Marching Home Again
in the classroom, as if a psalm,
as children, as novitiates in the Army
before the orders came.

Now, afternoons passing as the long mornings pass,
I merely stand at the window,
let children trample flower beds
searching for a lost ball, a glass-eyed marble.
Maybe once in our lives
we press through the mask
with words so pure they ring
as church bells on a morning
cold as Christmas. Remember how the clean,
pure blue of that early winter sky
matches the way we fit together
when our bodies press speechless
in the winter dark. It is the sacred interior of words
we enter, and when we leave—
the faces of words beam upon us,
our breath holds in the church, syllables
like motes of dust in the altar light.

Speech after long silence
seems the proper sequence,
but still, silence and the right words
are like lovers themselves intertwined,
twisting together season upon season

as a double helix performs its regenerating
dance, a copious resurrection:
self and other, other and self.

Absolute doubt like absolute zero
cannot be attained, cannot reach
a point where all movement is stayed.
Faith beyond reason is the same.
It is as if a few broken words
were at our core, and years
assemble them again only to find
we need them less and less.

We may as well just dwell in images,
each experiential mote
hung like paintings
on a museum wall.

Remember how your mother
brought orange-flavored aspirin
and water to your bed when you were sick,
a flower in a clear glass vase, pillows
plumped; you watched the bubbles on the stem
detach and rise and break
like words you never spoke
even as she lay dying,
the hospital cheerless despite
flowered wallpaper for the terminally ill.

How foolish to beg forgiveness
for words not said,
for all the words that were—
the gospel of our lives,

a psalm once sung, as if one's voice
could rise above the nave.

On the final days, the final words
spoken only to one's self
chosen carefully, as if afraid
they'll break like glass,
a crystal goblet fallen, breaking beautifully,
phonemes shattered in intricate patterns
leaving this world speechless
and articulate at the same time
as if watching a woman so dearly loved
slowly shed her evening-dress.

AFTER A READING OF WAR POEMS, THE SIGNING OF BOOKS

I've never been asked this before,
asked to inscribe a book
for someone who's dead.

I can barely deal with death
in the backyard, voles preyed on
by cats, a squirrel caught in a rain barrel:
late, late fall and water as cold
as the gnarled hand of death;
my hand freezes as I pull out
ice-stiff remains of squirrel.

It would take a month
of intense contemplation,
serious philosophical and theological
speculation on what would be done
with the book after it's signed

before I might come up with something
appropriate to say; I'm not a priest, not
a philosopher, not even human
half the time except when consumed
by anger, dreams of a holy vengeance.

Yes, the sacrament of revenge
defines me best and would give
this woman whose husband recently died

from wounds suffered in Vietnam,
wounds from decades ago, wounds
eating away every day of his life—solace?
A semblance of peace? Rectification
of wrongs? There is nothing I can offer:

anger and retribution a poor
compensation for loss such as hers.

Loss, it's been said, is the new poetic
philosophy, but that entails remembrance,
and therapists say
looking back is a time distortion, on
a displacement of events,

a danger, self-destructive
if one stays
for more than a fleeting moment
reliving and reliving like an image
mirrored in a mirror, endless
dispensations, causality just a jumble
of psychic debris.

Time is an art choreographed
by memory. This woman is beautiful,
lovely in her sincerity. I'm a flippant

SOB, an acerbic curmudgeon
insistent on a realistic appraisal
of everything. I have to work hard
at being nice in a world
where the bastards always win.

I want to write something,
anything
that will somehow ease or make sense
of her loss, but I know so little,
and empathy carries only so far.

The world spins from one war to another
as our gods play out their wrathful dreams.
I provide platitudes, nothing more,
hoping the small words will help.

I know what I wrote;
I can't say it to you.

THE CAT

OK, that's that. I look through
the *Condé Nast Traveler* magazine
and find there is no place I can go to
that I can afford. Not even
in the afterlife.

When I woke up feeling like
Schrödinger's cat, both alive
and dead at the same time,
I thought this a wonderful state,
a state where I know so little,
and yet the grandest matter
can be discerned through the simple
act of observation.

Merely have to look more closely at myself
and our shape-shifting,
spooky-action-at-a-distance world.

My eyes are a double slit experiment
in themselves.

And if I close my eyes I can feel
I am in two places at once,
two states of being—an action verb
and a state of being verb simultaneously.

I see the gate open and closed at the same time.

And why not? Why not be in two states
at once? Loving and not loving, happy and morose,
lively and sluggish as a lizard
in a blizzard. Funny and not in any way
funny at the same time.

Damn this life is fine—
though Schrödinger's wave equation
confuses my literary and unliterary mind
in equal and unequal undulating pulsations.

I shrug my shoulders and psi.

NOTES ON THE POEMS

YELLOW: Originally, when this poem was written, the following quote from a research article written by R. Latta was used as an epigraph: "Psychologically, a blind man in his circumstances lives in two worlds—the world as it would be if no one saw, and, in part at least, the world as the result of mental process in human beings who see." As an additional note here, R. L. Gregory studied the vision of a patient similar to those studied by Latta and wrote, ". . . his ideas of the world arose from touch. His general way of life as a blind man remained with him until his death." This patient, Gregory notes (somewhat disturbingly), ". . . had lost more than he had gained by recovery of sight."

FUBAR: To save the reader time and the effort involved in searching lists of military acronyms and the urban dictionary for abbreviations used in the poem, I have listed them as follows: TPFDL, Time-Phased Force Deployment List; STRAC, Strong, Tough, Ready Around the Clock (among other definitions); AMRAAM, Advanced Medium-Range Air-to-Air Missile; SIPRNET, Secret Internet Protocol Router Network; LSMFT, Lucky Strikes Mean Fine Tobacco, or, in the minds of adolescent boys growing up in the fifties, Loose Straps Mean Floppy (and you can fill in the last word here); TLDR, Too Long, Didn't Read; LQTM, Laughing Quietly To Myself; FFS:RTFM, For F**k's Sake: Read The F**king Manual; FODMAPS, Fermentable Oligosaccharides, Disaccharides, Monosaccharides and Polyols, (all carbohydrates poorly absorbed in the small intestine); IRL, In Real Life.

THE CAT: Psi, twenty-third letter of the Greek alphabet, symbol of Schrödinger's wave function. Not "pounds per square inch." Sigh.

www.ingramcontent.com/pod-product-compliance
Lightning Source LLC
LaVergne TN
LVHW041037150826
845672LV00001B/356

* 9 7 8 9 3 6 3 5 4 9 7 3 9 *